5
american popular piano
SKILLS

Created by
Dr. Scott
McBride Smith

Series Composer
Christopher
Norton

Editor
Dr. Scott
McBride Smith

Associate Editor
Clarke
MacIntosh

Book Design & Engraving
Andrew Jones

Cover Design
Wagner Design

Introduction

Everyone agrees that Tiger Woods is one of the greatest golfers of all time. Some even think he is the best ever! He won the 1997 Masters Tournament when he was 21 years old, the youngest winner in history. He was also the youngest golfer to complete a career *Grand Slam*, winning all four major championships by the age of 25.

How did he do it? Let's see what he says.

From early childhood I dreamed of being the world's best golfer. I worked hard and applied my family's values to everything I did. Integrity, honesty, discipline, responsiblity and fun; I learned these values at home and in school, each one pushing me further toward my dream.

Eldrick (Tiger) Woods
Letter from Tiger, Tiger Woods Foundation Website
http://www.twfound.org

The best way to achieve [a] goal is through sound fundamentals.

Tiger Woods
Golf Digest, November 1998

What's your dream? Do you want to be one of the world's best musicians? play piano for your own enjoyment? or entertain your friends and family? No matter which, Tiger is right. Hard work, responsibility – and fun! – will be the keystones to your success.

In golf, the term "fundamentals" covers many things. In piano playing, we can break it down into three broad groupings.

- ■ **Technic.** This is the ability to readily make the motions that create beautiful sounds. Dynamic control, tonal evenness and variety, and speed would fall into this category.

- ■ **Sightreading.** You might also call these "quick learning" skills. Seeing patterns, noticing details, and playing without stopping – right away.

- ■ **Listening.** This is perhaps the most important of all! If you can't hear the sounds of a piece in your mind before you play, you will never do a good job performing it. Psychologists call this "audiation".

Do you think practicing basic skills is boring? Get over it!

Your playing will never be as good or as enjoyable as you want it to be if your basic skills are not excellent. Every athlete – including Tiger – spends time on drills, exercises and warm-ups outside of the game. Pianists should, too. When your piano fundamentals become strong, you will learn everything more easily and perform more confidently.

This book is designed to help, but it won't work if you don't! Practice carefully and frequently. Spend some time every day on your basic skills and, who knows ... you may become the Tiger Woods of the piano.

Library and Archives Canada Cataloguing in Publication

Smith, Scott McBride

American popular piano [music] : skills / created by Scott McBride Smith ;
series composer, Christopher Norton ;
editor, Scott McBride Smith ; associate editor, Clarke MacIntosh.

To be complete in 11 volumes.
Publisher's nos.: APP S-00 (level P); APP S-01 (level 1); APP S-02 (level 2).
Contents: Preparatory level -- Level 1 -- Level 2.
Miscellaneous information: The series is organized in 11 levels, from preparatory to level 10, each including a repertoire album, an etudes album, a skills book, a "technic" book, and an instrumental backings compact disc.

ISBN 978-1-897379-22-6 (preparatory level).--ISBN 978-1-897379-23-3 (level 1).--
ISBN 978-1-897379-24-0 (level 2).--ISBN 978-1-897379-25-7 (level 3).--
ISBN 978-1-897379-26-4 (level 4).--ISBN 978-1-897379-27-1 (level 5)

1. Piano--Studies and exercises. 2. Piano--Studies and exercises--Juvenile.
I. Norton, Christopher, 1953- II. MacIntosh, S. Clarke, 1959- III. Title.

LEVEL 5 SKILLS

Table of Contents

Introduction ii

Skills Modules

Unit 1
  Module 1 2
  Module 2 4
  Module 3 6
  Module 4 8

Unit 2
  Module 1 10
  Module 2 12
  Module 3 14
  Module 4 16

Unit 3
  Module 1 18
  Module 2 20
  Module 3 22
  Module 4 24

Unit 4
  Module 1 26
  Module 2 28
  Module 3 30
  Module 4 32

Skills Tests

Unit 1
  Midterm 34
  Final 35

Unit 2
  Midterm 36
  Final 37

Unit 3
  Midterm 38
  Final 39

Unit 4
  Midterm 40
  Final 41

Technic

  Scales 42
  Chords 44
  Arpeggios 46
  Mixolydian Modes & Licks 47
  Drills 48

How to Use this Book 50

Technic Tracker .... inside back cover

Unit One - Module One

A. Technic

Set weekly practice schedule as assigned by your teacher. For directions, see *How to Use This Book* on page 50.

1) Chords (pages 44-45)

No.(s) _____ ;

M.M. ♩ = _____ ;

key(s): C G D c

2) Arpeggios (page 46)

No.(s) _____ ;

M.M. ♩ = _____ ;

key(s): E♭ A♭ D♭

3) Drills (pages 48-49)

No.(s) _____ ;

M.M. ♩ = _____ ;

key(s): G D

4) Mixolydian Modes (page

No.(s) _____ ;

M.M. ♩ = _____ ;

on: C F B♭

5) Scales (pages 42-43)

No.(s) _____ ;

M.M. ♩ = _____ ;

key(s): C G D c

Articulation:

  legato   *staccato*   *portato*

Dynamic:

  𝆑   𝆏   *mf*   *mp*   *ff*   *pp*

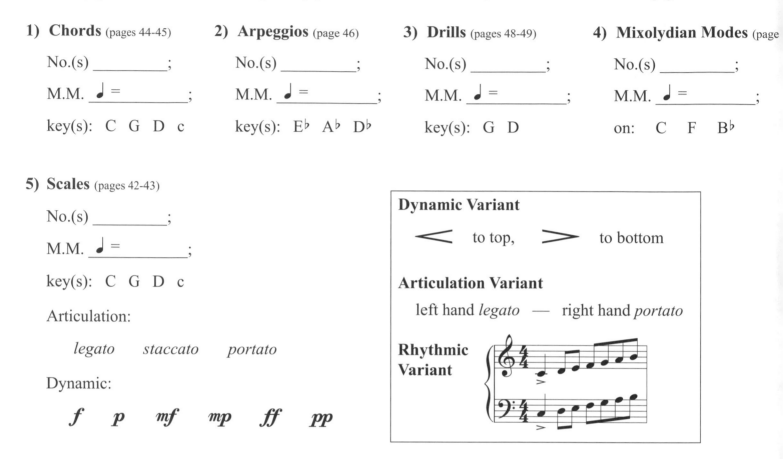

Dynamic Variant

⟨ to top,   ⟩ to bottom

Articulation Variant

left hand *legato* — right hand *portato*

Rhythmic Variant

B. Prepared Sightreading Piece

Play at least three times each week. Keep a steady beat.

For directions, see *How to Use This Book* on page 50.

C. Aural Skills - Rhythmic   For directions, see *How to Use This Book* on page 50.

Tap each exercise with the backing track to *The Showman* while counting out loud.
- start with the Practice track, progress to the Performance track
- make bigger gestures for the accented notes, smaller gestures for unaccented ones.

i)   First tap the lower rhythm on your left thigh.
ii) Then tap the top rhythm on your right thigh.
iii) Finally tap both rhythms, hands together.

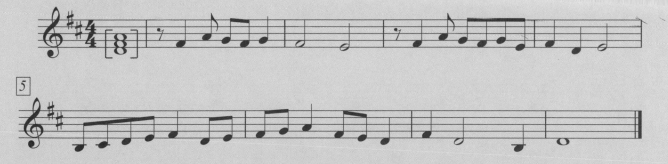

a)

b)

c)

D. Aural Skills - Pitch   For directions, see *How to Use This Book* on page 50.

1) Sing and play the phrase simultaneously. Repeat, but don't play the last two bars – just sing them. Finally, just sing the entire phrase.

2) Sing the top part while playing only the bass line at the piano.

Unit One - Module Two

A. Technic

Set weekly practice schedule as assigned by your teacher. For directions, see *How to Use This Book* on page 50.

1) Chords (pages 44-45)

No.(s) _____ ;

M.M. ♩ = _____ ;

key(s): C G D c

2) Arpeggios (page 46)

No.(s) _____ ;

M.M. ♩ = _____ ;

key(s): E♭ A♭ D♭

3) Drills (pages 48-49)

No.(s) _____ ;

M.M. ♩ = _____ ;

key(s): G D

4) Mixolydian Modes (page

No.(s) _____ ;

M.M. ♩ = _____ ;

on: C F B♭

5) Scales (pages 42-43)

No.(s) _____ ;

M.M. ♩ = _____ ;

key(s): C G D c

Articulation:

  legato   staccato   portato

Dynamic:

  f   p   mf   mp   ff   pp

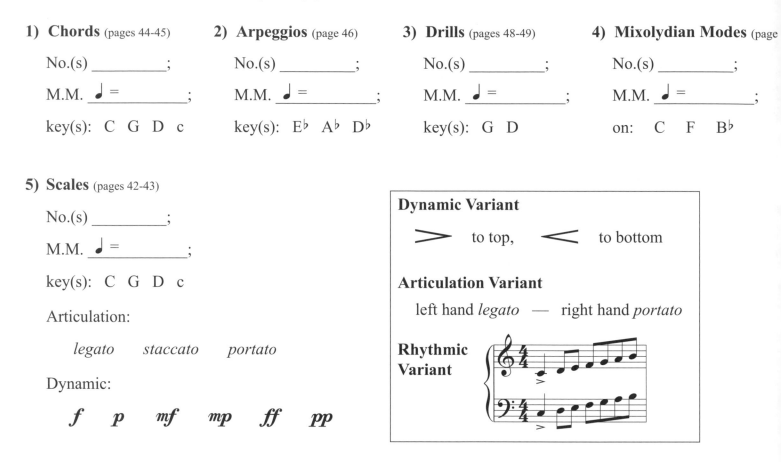

Dynamic Variant

> to top, < to bottom

Articulation Variant

left hand *legato* — right hand *portato*

Rhythmic Variant

B. Prepared Sightreading Piece

Play at least three times each week. Keep a steady beat.

For directions, see *How to Use This Book* on page 50.

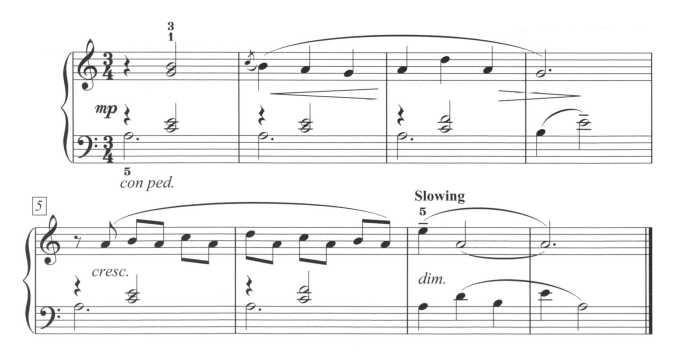

C. Aural Skills - Rhythmic For directions, see *How to Use This Book* on page 50.

Tap each exercise with the backing track to *Fly Me Away* while counting a swung ♪ pulse out loud.
- start with the Practice track, progress to the Performance track
- make bigger gestures for the accented notes, smaller gestures for unaccented ones.

   i) First tap the lower rhythm on your left thigh.
   ii) Then tap the top rhythm on your right thigh.
   iii) Finally tap both rhythms, hands together.

a)

b)

c)

D. Aural Skills - Pitch For directions, see *How to Use This Book* on page 50.

1) Sing and play the phrase simultaneously. Repeat, but don't play the last two bars – just sing them. Finally, just sing the entire phrase.

2) Sing the top part while playing only the bass line at the piano.

Unit One - Module Three

A. Technic

Set weekly practice schedule as assigned by your teacher. For directions, see *How to Use This Book* on page 50.

1) Chords (pages 44-45)

No.(s) _____;

M.M. ♩ = _____;

key(s): C G D c

2) Arpeggios (page 46)

No.(s) _____;

M.M. ♩ = _____;

key(s): E♭ A♭ D♭

3) Drills (pages 48-49)

No.(s) _____;

M.M. ♩ = _____;

key(s): G D

4) Mixolydian Modes (page 4

No.(s) _____;

M.M. ♩ = _____;

on: C F B♭

5) Scales (pages 42-43)

No.(s) _____;

M.M. ♩ = _____;

key(s): C G D c

Articulation:

legato   staccato   portato

Dynamic:

f   p   mf   mp   ff   pp

Dynamic Variant

left hand *p* — right hand *f*

Articulation Variant

left hand *legato* — right hand *portato*

Rhythmic Variant

B. Prepared Sightreading Piece

Play at least three times each week. Keep a steady beat.

For directions, see *How to Use This Book* on page 50.

C. Aural Skills - Rhythmic

For directions, see *How to Use This Book* on page 50.

Tap each exercise with the backing track to *Back on Holiday* while counting out loud.
- start with the Practice track, progress to the Performance track
- make bigger gestures for the accented notes, smaller gestures for unaccented ones.

    i) First tap the lower rhythm on your left thigh.
    ii) Then tap the top rhythm on your right thigh.
    iii) Finally tap both rhythms, hands together.

D. Aural Skills - Pitch

For directions, see *How to Use This Book* on page 50.

1) Sing and play the phrase simultaneously. Repeat, but don't play the last two bars – just sing them. Finally, just sing the entire phrase.

2) Sing the top part while playing only the bass line at the piano.

Unit One - Module Four

A. Technic

Set weekly practice schedule as assigned by your teacher. For directions, see *How to Use This Book* on page 50.

1) Chords (pages 44-45)

No.(s) _____ ;

M.M. ♩ = _____ ;

key(s): C G D c

2) Arpeggios (page 46)

No.(s) _____ ;

M.M. ♩ = _____ ;

key(s): E♭ A♭ D♭

3) Drills (pages 48-49)

No.(s) _____ ;

M.M. ♩ = _____ ;

key(s): G D

4) Mixolydian Modes (page 4

No.(s) _____ ;

M.M. ♩ = _____ ;

on: C F B♭

5) Scales (pages 42-43)

No.(s) _____ ;

M.M. ♩ = _____ ;

key(s): C G D c

Articulation:

legato   staccato   portato

Dynamic:

f   *p*   *mf*   *mp*   *ff*   *pp*

Dynamic Variant

left hand *f* — right hand *p*

Articulation Variant

left hand *legato* — right hand *portato*

Rhythmic Variant

B. Prepared Sightreading Piece

Play at least three times each week. Keep a steady beat.

For directions, see *How to Use This Book* on page 50.

C. Aural Skills - Rhythmic   For directions, see *How to Use This Book* on page 50.

Tap each exercise with the backing track to *Floating Away* while counting out loud.
- start with the Practice track, progress to the Performance track
- make bigger gestures for the accented notes, smaller gestures for unaccented ones.

   i)   First tap the lower rhythm on your left thigh.
   ii) Then tap the top rhythm on your right thigh.
   iii) Finally tap both rhythms, hands together.

a)

b)

c)

D. Aural Skills - Pitch   For directions, see *How to Use This Book* on page 50.

1) Sing and play the phrase simultaneously. Repeat, but don't play the last two bars – just sing them. Finally, just sing the entire phrase.

2) Sing the top part while playing only the bass line at the piano.

Unit Two - Module One

A. Technic

Set weekly practice schedule as assigned by your teacher. For directions, see *How to Use This Book* on page 50.

1) Chords (pages 44-45)

No.(s) _____ ;

M.M. ♩ = _____ ;

key(s): D c g A

2) Arpeggios (page 46)

No.(s) _____ ;

M.M. ♩ = _____ ;

key(s): A♭ D♭ f♯

3) Drills (pages 48-49)

No.(s) _____ ;

M.M. ♩ = _____ ;

key(s): E B

4) Mixolydian Modes (page 4

No.(s) _____ ;

M.M. ♩ = _____ ;

on: F B♭ G

5) Scales (pages 42-43)

No.(s) _____ ;

M.M. ♩ = _____ ;

key(s): D c g A

Articulation:

legato   staccato   portato

Dynamic:

f   p   mf   mp   ff   pp

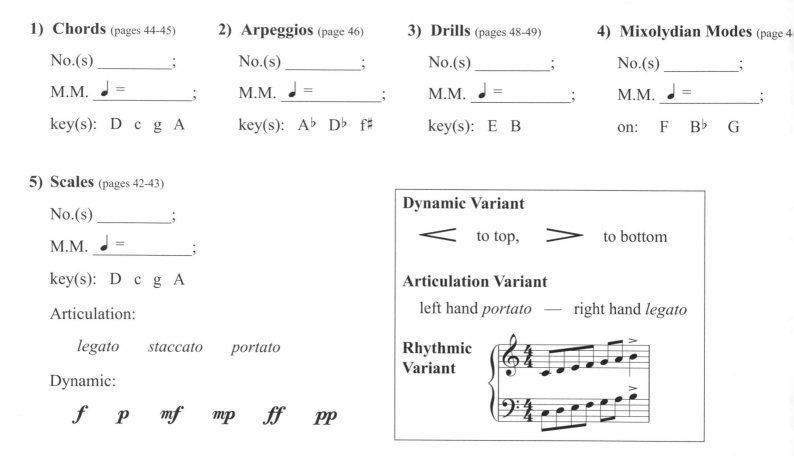

Dynamic Variant

< to top,   > to bottom

Articulation Variant

left hand *portato* — right hand *legato*

Rhythmic Variant

B. Prepared Sightreading Piece

Play at least three times each week. Keep a steady beat.

For directions, see *How to Use This Book* on page 50.

C. Aural Skills - Rhythmic   For directions, see *How to Use This Book* on page 50.

Tap each exercise with the backing track to *Fly Me Away* while counting a swung ♪ pulse out loud.
- start with the Practice track, progress to the Performance track
- make bigger gestures for the accented notes,

smaller gestures for unaccented ones.
- i) First tap the lower rhythm on your left thigh.
- ii) Then tap the top rhythm on your right thigh.
- iii) Finally tap both rhythms, hands together.

a)
b)
c)

D. Aural Skills - Pitch   For directions, see *How to Use This Book* on page 50.

1) Sing and play the phrase simultaneously. Repeat, but don't play the last two bars – just sing them. Finally, just sing the entire phrase.

2) Sing the top part while playing only the bass line at the piano.

Unit Two - Module Two

A. Technic

Set weekly practice schedule as assigned by your teacher. For directions, see *How to Use This Book* on page 50.

1) Chords (pages 44-45)

No.(s) _____;

M.M. ♩ = _____;

key(s): D   c   g   A

2) Arpeggios (page 46)

No.(s) _____;

M.M. ♩ = _____;

key(s): A♭   D♭   f♯

3) Drills (pages 48-49)

No.(s) _____;

M.M. ♩ = _____;

key(s): E   B

4) Mixolydian Modes (page

No.(s) _____;

M.M. ♩ = _____;

on: F   B♭   G

5) Scales (pages 42-43)

No.(s) _____;

M.M. ♩ = _____;

key(s): D   c   g   A

Articulation:

legato   *staccato*   *portato*

Dynamic:

f   *p*   *mf*   *mp*   *ff*   *pp*

Dynamic Variant

> to top,   < to bottom

Articulation Variant

left hand *portato* — right hand *legato*

Rhythmic Variant

B. Prepared Sightreading Piece

Play at least three times each week. Keep a steady beat.

For directions, see *How to Use This Book* on page 50.

C. Aural Skills - Rhythmic   For directions, see *How to Use This Book* on page 50.

Tap each exercise with the backing track to *Floating Away* while counting out loud.
- start with the Practice track, progress to the Performance track
- make bigger gestures for the accented notes,

smaller gestures for unaccented ones.
- i)   First tap the lower rhythm on your left thigh.
- ii) Then tap the top rhythm on your right thigh.
- iii) Finally tap both rhythms, hands together.

a)

b)

c)

D. Aural Skills - Pitch   For directions, see *How to Use This Book* on page 50.

1) Sing and play the phrase simultaneously. Repeat, but don't play the last two bars – just sing them. Finally, just sing the entire phrase.

2) Sing the top part while playing only the bass line at the piano.

14

Unit Two - Module Three

A. Technic

Set weekly practice schedule as assigned by your teacher. For directions, see *How to Use This Book* on page 50.

1) Chords (pages 44-45)

No.(s) _____ ;

M.M. ♩ = _____ ;

key(s): D c g A

2) Arpeggios (page 46)

No.(s) _____ ;

M.M. ♩ = _____ ;

key(s): A♭ D♭ f♯

3) Drills (pages 48-49)

No.(s) _____ ;

M.M. ♩ = _____ ;

key(s): E B

4) Mixolydian Modes (page

No.(s) _____ ;

M.M. ♩ = _____ ;

on: F B♭ G

5) Scales (pages 42-43)

No.(s) _____ ;

M.M. ♩ = _____ ;

key(s): D c g A

Articulation:

 legato   staccato   portato

Dynamic:

 f   p   mf   mp   ff   pp

> **Dynamic Variant**
>
> left hand *p* — right hand *f*
>
> **Articulation Variant**
>
> left hand *portato* — right hand *legato*
>
> **Rhythmic Variant**

B. Prepared Sightreading Piece

Play at least three times each week. Keep a steady beat.

For directions, see *How to Use This Book* on page 50.

C. Aural Skills - Rhythmic

For directions, see *How to Use This Book* on page 50.

Tap each exercise with the backing track to *Back on Holiday* while counting out loud.
- start with the Practice track, progress to the Performance track
- make bigger gestures for the accented notes, smaller gestures for unaccented ones.

i) First tap the lower rhythm on your left thigh.
ii) Then tap the top rhythm on your right thigh.
iii) Finally tap both rhythms, hands together.

a)

b)

c)

D. Aural Skills - Pitch

For directions, see *How to Use This Book* on page 50.

1) Sing and play the phrase simultaneously. Repeat, but don't play the last two bars – just sing them. Finally, just sing the entire phrase.

2) Sing the top part while playing only the bass line at the piano.

Unit Two - Module Four

A. Technic

Set weekly practice schedule as assigned by your teacher. For directions, see *How to Use This Book* on page 50.

1) Chords (pages 44-45)

No.(s) _____;

M.M. ♩ = _____;

key(s): D c g A

2) Arpeggios (page 46)

No.(s) _____;

M.M. ♩ = _____;

key(s): A♭ D♭ f♯

3) Drills (pages 48-49)

No.(s) _____;

M.M. ♩ = _____;

key(s): E B

4) Mixolydian Modes (page 4

No.(s) _____;

M.M. ♩ = _____;

on: F B♭ G

5) Scales (pages 42-43)

No.(s) _____;

M.M. ♩ = _____;

key(s): D c g A

Articulation:

legato   staccato   portato

Dynamic:

f   p   mf   mp   ff   pp

Dynamic Variant

left hand *f* — right hand *p*

Articulation Variant

left hand *portato* — right hand *legato*

Rhythmic Variant

B. Prepared Sightreading Piece

Play at least three times each week. Keep a steady beat.

For directions, see *How to Use This Book* on page 50.

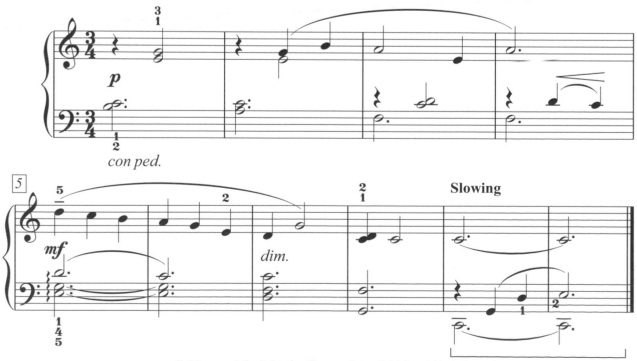

C. Aural Skills - Rhythmic   For directions, see *How to Use This Book* on page 50.

Tap each exercise with the backing track to *The Showman* while counting out loud.
- start with the Practice track, progress to the Performance track
- make bigger gestures for the accented notes,

smaller gestures for unaccented ones.

i)   First tap the lower rhythm on your left thigh.
ii) Then tap the top rhythm on your right thigh.
iii) Finally tap both rhythms, hands together.

a)

b)

c)

D. Aural Skills - Pitch   For directions, see *How to Use This Book* on page 50.

1) Sing and play the phrase simultaneously. Repeat, but don't play the last two bars – just sing them. Finally, just sing the entire phrase.

2) Sing the top part while playing only the bass line at the piano.

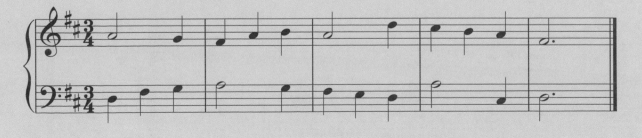

Unit Three - Module One

A. Technic

Set weekly practice schedule as assigned by your teacher. For directions, see *How to Use This Book* on page 50.

1) Chords (pages 44-45)

No.(s) _____ ;

M.M. ♩ = _____ ;

key(s): g A E d

2) Arpeggios (page 46)

No.(s) _____ ;

M.M. ♩ = _____ ;

key(s): D♭ f♯ c♯

3) Drills (pages 48-49)

No.(s) _____ ;

M.M. ♩ = _____ ;

key(s): B♭ E♭

4) Mixolydian Modes (page 4?)

No.(s) _____ ;

M.M. ♩ = _____ ;

on: B♭ G D

5) Scales (pages 42-43)

No.(s) _____ ;

M.M. ♩ = _____ ;

key(s): g A E d

Articulation:

legato   staccato   portato

Dynamic:

f   p   mf   mp   ff   pp

> **Dynamic Variant**
>
> < to top,   > to bottom
>
> **Articulation Variant**
>
> left hand *portato* — right hand *legato*
>
> **Rhythmic Variant**

B. Prepared Sightreading Piece

For directions, see *How to Use This Book* on page 50.

Play at least three times each week. Keep a steady beat.

C. Aural Skills - Rhythmic   For directions, see *How to Use This Book* on page 50.

Tap each exercise with the backing track to *Back on Holiday* while counting out loud.
- start with the Practice track, progress to the Performance track
- make bigger gestures for the accented notes,

smaller gestures for unaccented ones.
  i)   First tap the lower rhythm on your left thigh.
  ii) Then tap the top rhythm on your right thigh.
  iii) Finally tap both rhythms, hands together.

a)

b)

c)

D. Aural Skills - Pitch   For directions, see *How to Use This Book* on page 50.

1) Sing and play the phrase simultaneously. Repeat, but don't play the last two bars – just sing them. Finally, just sing the entire phrase.

swung 8ths

2) Sing the top part while playing only the bass line at the piano.

Unit Three - Module Two

A. Technic

Set weekly practice schedule as assigned by your teacher. For directions, see *How to Use This Book* on page 50.

1) Chords (pages 44-45)

No.(s) _____ ;

M.M. ♩ = _____ ;

key(s): g A E d

2) Arpeggios (page 46)

No.(s) _____ ;

M.M. ♩ = _____ ;

key(s): D♭ f♯ c♯

3) Drills (pages 48-49)

No.(s) _____ ;

M.M. ♩ = _____ ;

key(s): B♭ E♭

4) Mixolydian Modes (page 4

No.(s) _____ ;

M.M. ♩ = _____ ;

on: B♭ G D

5) Scales (pages 42-43)

No.(s) _____ ;

M.M. ♩ = _____ ;

key(s): g A E d

Articulation:

    legato   *staccato*   *portato*

Dynamic:

    f   *p*   *mf*   *mp*   *ff*   *pp*

Dynamic Variant

> to top,   < to bottom

Articulation Variant

left hand *portato* — right hand *legato*

Rhythmic Variant

B. Prepared Sightreading Piece

Play at least three times each week. Keep a steady beat.

For directions, see *How to Use This Book* on page 50.

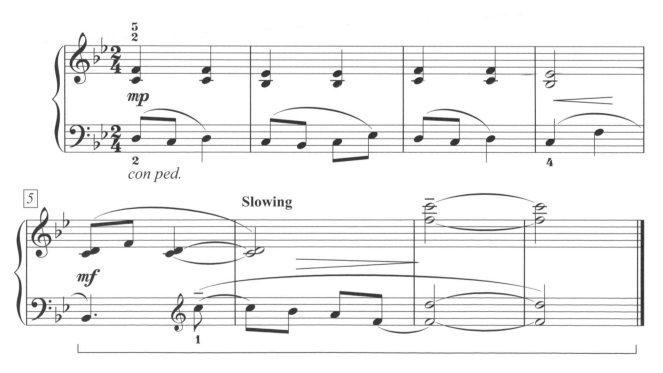

C. Aural Skills - Rhythmic   For directions, see *How to Use This Book* on page 50.

Tap each exercise with the backing track to *The Showman* while counting out loud.
- start with the Practice track, progress to the Performance track
- make bigger gestures for the accented notes, smaller gestures for unaccented ones.
    - i)   First tap the lower rhythm on your left thigh.
    - ii) Then tap the top rhythm on your right thigh.
    - iii) Finally tap both rhythms, hands together.

a)

b)

c)

D. Aural Skills - Pitch   For directions, see *How to Use This Book* on page 50.

1) Sing and play the phrase simultaneously. Repeat, but don't play the last two bars – just sing them. Finally, just sing the entire phrase.

2) Sing the top part while playing only the bass line at the piano.

Unit Three - Module Three

A. Technic

Set weekly practice schedule as assigned by your teacher. For directions, see *How to Use This Book* on page 50.

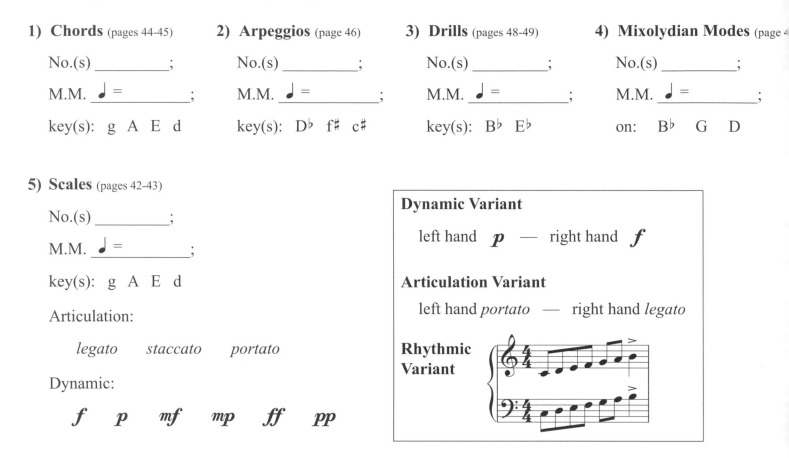

1) Chords (pages 44-45)

No.(s) _____ ;

M.M. ♩ = _____ ;

key(s): g A E d

2) Arpeggios (page 46)

No.(s) _____ ;

M.M. ♩ = _____ ;

key(s): D♭ f♯ c♯

3) Drills (pages 48-49)

No.(s) _____ ;

M.M. ♩ = _____ ;

key(s): B♭ E♭

4) Mixolydian Modes (page 4

No.(s) _____ ;

M.M. ♩ = _____ ;

on: B♭ G D

5) Scales (pages 42-43)

No.(s) _____ ;

M.M. ♩ = _____ ;

key(s): g A E d

Articulation:

    legato   *staccato*   *portato*

Dynamic:

    f   *p*   *mf*   *mp*   *ff*   *pp*

Dynamic Variant

    left hand *p* — right hand *f*

Articulation Variant

    left hand *portato* — right hand *legato*

Rhythmic Variant

B. Prepared Sightreading Piece

Play at least three times each week. Keep a steady beat.

For directions, see *How to Use This Book* on page 50.

C. Aural Skills - Rhythmic

For directions, see *How to Use This Book* on page 50.

Tap each exercise with the backing track to *Floating Away* while counting out loud.
- start with the Practice track, progress to the Performance track
- make bigger gestures for the accented notes, smaller gestures for unaccented ones.

i) First tap the lower rhythm on your left thigh.
ii) Then tap the top rhythm on your right thigh.
iii) Finally tap both rhythms, hands together.

D. Aural Skills - Pitch

For directions, see *How to Use This Book* on page 50.

1) Sing and play the phrase simultaneously. Repeat, but don't play the last two bars – just sing them. Finally, just sing the entire phrase.

2) Sing the top part while playing only the bass line at the piano.

24

Unit Three - Module Four

A. Technic

Set weekly practice schedule as assigned by your teacher. For directions, see *How to Use This Book* on page 50.

1) Chords (pages 44-45)

No.(s) _____;

M.M. ♩ = _____;

key(s): g A E d

2) Arpeggios (page 46)

No.(s) _____;

M.M. ♩ = _____;

key(s): D♭ f♯ c♯

3) Drills (pages 48-49)

No.(s) _____;

M.M. ♩ = _____;

key(s): B♭ E♭

4) Mixolydian Modes (page 4?)

No.(s) _____;

M.M. ♩ = _____;

on: B♭ G D

5) Scales (pages 42-43)

No.(s) _____;

M.M. ♩ = _____;

key(s): g A E d

Articulation:

　legato　　*staccato*　　*portato*

Dynamic:

　f　*p*　*mf*　*mp*　*ff*　*pp*

Dynamic Variant

left hand *f* — right hand *p*

Articulation Variant

left hand *portato* — right hand *legato*

Rhythmic Variant

B. Prepared Sightreading Piece

Play at least three times each week. Keep a steady beat.

For directions, see *How to Use This Book* on page 50.

C. Aural Skills - Rhythmic   For directions, see *How to Use This Book* on page 50.

Tap each exercise with the backing track to *Fly Me Away* while counting a swung ♪ pulse out loud.
- start with the Practice track, progress to the Performance track
- make bigger gestures for the accented notes, smaller gestures for unaccented ones.
    - i)   First tap the lower rhythm on your left thigh.
    - ii) Then tap the top rhythm on your right thigh.
    - iii) Finally tap both rhythms, hands together.

a)

b)

c)

D. Aural Skills - Pitch   For directions, see *How to Use This Book* on page 50.

1) Sing and play the phrase simultaneously. Repeat, but don't play the last two bars – just sing them. Finally, just sing the entire phrase.

2) Sing the top part while playing only the bass line at the piano.

Unit Four - Module One

A. Technic

Set weekly practice schedule as assigned by your teacher. For directions, see *How to Use This Book* on page 50.

1) Chords (pages 44-45)

No.(s) _____ ;

M.M. ♩ = _____ ;

key(s): E d E♭ f

2) Arpeggios (page 46)

No.(s) _____ ;

M.M. ♩ = _____ ;

key(s): f♯ c♯ g♯

3) Drills (pages 48-49)

No.(s) _____ ;

M.M. ♩ = _____ ;

key(s): A♭ G♭

4) Mixolydian Modes (page 4

No.(s) _____ ;

M.M. ♩ = _____ ;

on: G   D   A

5) Scales (pages 42-43)

No.(s) _____ ;

M.M. ♩ = _____ ;

key(s): E d E♭ f

Articulation:

legato   staccato   portato

Dynamic:

𝆑   𝆏   𝆐𝆑   𝆐𝆏   𝆑𝆑   𝆏𝆏

Dynamic Variant

< to top,   > to bottom

Articulation Variant

left hand *legato* — right hand *portato*

Rhythmic Variant

B. Prepared Sightreading Piece

Play at least three times each week. Keep a steady beat.

For directions, see *How to Use This Book* on page 50.

C. Aural Skills - Rhythmic

For directions, see *How to Use This Book* on page 50.

Tap each exercise with the backing track to *Floating Away* while counting out loud.
- start with the Practice track, progress to the Performance track
- make bigger gestures for the accented notes,

smaller gestures for unaccented ones.

i) First tap the lower rhythm on your left thigh.
ii) Then tap the top rhythm on your right thigh.
iii) Finally tap both rhythms, hands together.

a)

b)

c)

D. Aural Skills - Pitch

For directions, see *How to Use This Book* on page 50.

1) Sing and play the phrase simultaneously. Repeat, but don't play the last two bars – just sing them. Finally, just sing the entire phrase.

2) Sing the top part while playing only the bass line at the piano.

Unit Four - Module Two

A. Technic

Set weekly practice schedule as assigned by your teacher. For directions, see *How to Use This Book* on page 50.

1) Chords (pages 44-45)

No.(s) _____;

M.M. ♩ = _____;

key(s): E d E♭ f

2) Arpeggios (page 46)

No.(s) _____;

M.M. ♩ = _____;

key(s): f♯ c♯ g♯

3) Drills (pages 48-49)

No.(s) _____;

M.M. ♩ = _____;

key(s): A♭ G♭

4) Mixolydian Modes (page 4?)

No.(s) _____;

M.M. ♩ = _____;

on: G D A

5) Scales (pages 42-43)

No.(s) _____;

M.M. ♩ = _____;

key(s): E d E♭ f

Articulation:

   legato   staccato   portato

Dynamic:

f   p   mf   mp   ff   pp

Dynamic Variant

 > to top,   < to bottom

Articulation Variant

left hand *legato* — right hand *portato*

Rhythmic Variant

B. Prepared Sightreading Piece

Play at least three times each week. Keep a steady beat.

For directions, see *How to Use This Book* on page 50.

C. Aural Skills - Rhythmic   For directions, see *How to Use This Book* on page 50.

Tap each exercise with the backing track to *Back on Holiday* while counting out loud.
- start with the Practice track, progress to the Performance track
- make bigger gestures for the accented notes,

smaller gestures for unaccented ones.
- i) First tap the lower rhythm on your left thigh.
- ii) Then tap the top rhythm on your right thigh.
- iii) Finally tap both rhythms, hands together.

D. Aural Skills - Pitch   For directions, see *How to Use This Book* on page 50.

1) Sing and play the phrase simultaneously. Repeat, but don't play the last two bars – just sing them. Finally, just sing the entire phrase.

2) Sing the top part while playing only the bass line at the piano.

Unit Four - Module Three

A. Technic

Set weekly practice schedule as assigned by your teacher. For directions, see *How to Use This Book* on page 50.

1) Chords (pages 44-45)

No.(s) _____;

M.M. ♩ = _____;

key(s): E d E♭ f

2) Arpeggios (page 46)

No.(s) _____;

M.M. ♩ = _____;

key(s): f♯ c♯ g♯

3) Drills (pages 48-49)

No.(s) _____;

M.M. ♩ = _____;

key(s): A♭ G♭

4) Mixolydian Modes (page 47)

No.(s) _____;

M.M. ♩ = _____;

on: G D A

5) Scales (pages 42-43)

No.(s) _____;

M.M. ♩ = _____;

key(s): E d E♭ f

Articulation:

legato   *staccato*   *portato*

Dynamic:

f   *p*   *mf*   *mp*   *ff*   *pp*

Dynamic Variant

left hand *p* — right hand *f*

Articulation Variant

left hand *legato* — right hand *portato*

Rhythmic Variant

B. Prepared Sightreading Piece

Play at least three times each week. Keep a steady beat.

For directions, see *How to Use This Book* on page 50.

C. Aural Skills - Rhythmic   For directions, see *How to Use This Book* on page 50.

Tap each exercise with the backing track to *The Showman* while counting out loud.
- start with the Practice track, progress to the Performance track
- make bigger gestures for the accented notes,

smaller gestures for unaccented ones.

   i)   First tap the lower rhythm on your left thigh.
   ii) Then tap the top rhythm on your right thigh.
   iii) Finally tap both rhythms, hands together.

a)

b)

c)

D. Aural Skills - Pitch   For directions, see *How to Use This Book* on page 50.

1) Sing and play the phrase simultaneously. Repeat, but don't play the last two bars – just sing them. Finally, just sing the entire phrase.

2) Sing the top part while playing only the bass line at the piano.

Unit Four - Module Four

A. Technic

Set weekly practice schedule as assigned by your teacher. For directions, see *How to Use This Book* on page 50.

1) Chords (pages 44-45)

No.(s) ________;

M.M. ♩ = ________;

key(s): E d E♭ f

2) Arpeggios (page 46)

No.(s) ________;

M.M. ♩ = ________;

key(s): f♯ c♯ g♯

3) Drills (pages 48-49)

No.(s) ________;

M.M. ♩ = ________;

key(s): A♭ G♭

4) Mixolydian Modes (page

No.(s) ________;

M.M. ♩ = ________;

on: G D A

5) Scales (pages 42-43)

No.(s) ________;

M.M. ♩ = ________;

key(s): E d E♭ f

Articulation:

legato *staccato* *portato*

Dynamic:

f ***p*** ***mf*** ***mp*** ***ff*** ***pp***

Dynamic Variant

left hand ***f*** — right hand ***p***

Articulation Variant

left hand *legato* — right hand *portato*

Rhythmic Variant

B. Prepared Sightreading Piece

Play at least three times each week. Keep a steady beat.

For directions, see *How to Use This Book* on page 50.

C. Aural Skills - Rhythmic For directions, see *How to Use This Book* on page 50.

Tap each exercise with the backing track to *Fly Me Away* while counting a swung ♪ pulse out loud.

- start with the Practice track, progress to the Performance track
- make bigger gestures for the accented notes, smaller gestures for unaccented ones.
  i)   First tap the lower rhythm on your left thigh.
  ii) Then tap the top rhythm on your right thigh.
  iii) Finally tap both rhythms, hands together.

a)

b)

c)

D. Aural Skills - Pitch For directions, see *How to Use This Book* on page 50.

1) Sing and play the phrase simultaneously. Repeat, but don't play the last two bars – just sing them. Finally, just sing the entire phrase.

2) Sing the top part while playing only the bass line at the piano.

Unit 1 - Midterm

I. Technic   Grade [   ]

A. Chords
No.(s) _____ ; key(s) _____ ; M.M. _____ ;

B. Arpeggios
No.(s) _____ ; key(s) _____ ; M.M. _____ ;

C. Mixolydian Modes
No.(s) _____ ;   on _____ ; M.M. _____ ;

D. Drills
No.(s) _____ ; key(s) _____ ; M.M. _____ ;

E. Scales
No.(s) _____ ; key(s) _____ ; M.M. _____ ;

II. Sightreading   Grade [   ]   Student may study for up to 15 seconds.

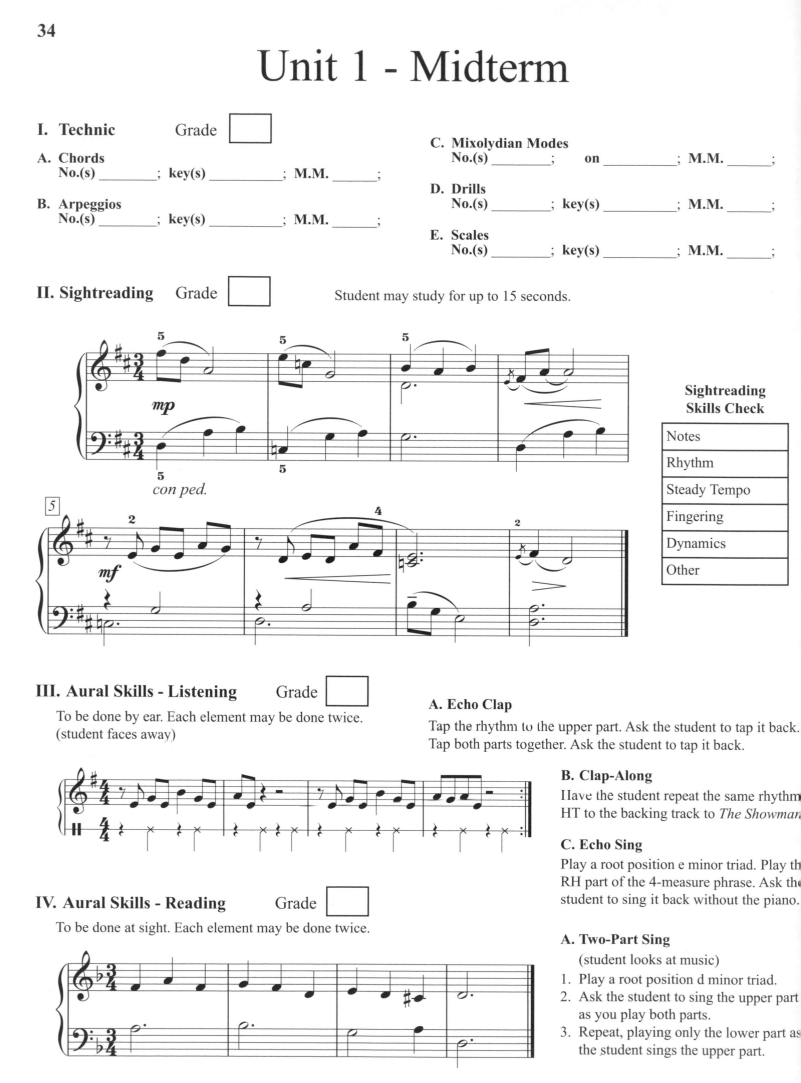

Sightreading Skills Check

Notes
Rhythm
Steady Tempo
Fingering
Dynamics
Other

III. Aural Skills - Listening   Grade [   ]

To be done by ear. Each element may be done twice.
(student faces away)

A. Echo Clap

Tap the rhythm to the upper part. Ask the student to tap it back.
Tap both parts together. Ask the student to tap it back.

B. Clap-Along

Have the student repeat the same rhythm
HT to the backing track to *The Showma*

C. Echo Sing

Play a root position e minor triad. Play th
RH part of the 4-measure phrase. Ask the
student to sing it back without the piano.

IV. Aural Skills - Reading   Grade [   ]

To be done at sight. Each element may be done twice.

A. Two-Part Sing

(student looks at music)
1. Play a root position d minor triad.
2. Ask the student to sing the upper part
   as you play both parts.
3. Repeat, playing only the lower part as
   the student sings the upper part.

Unit 1 - Final

I. Technic Grade ☐

A. Chords
No.(s) _____ ; key(s) _____ ; M.M. _____ ;

B. Arpeggios
No.(s) _____ ; key(s) _____ ; M.M. _____ ;

C. Mixolydian Modes
No.(s) _____ ; on _____ ; M.M. _____ ;

D. Drills
No.(s) _____ ; key(s) _____ ; M.M. _____ ;

E. Scales
No.(s) _____ ; key(s) _____ ; M.M. _____ ;

II. Sightreading Grade ☐   Student may study for up to 15 seconds.

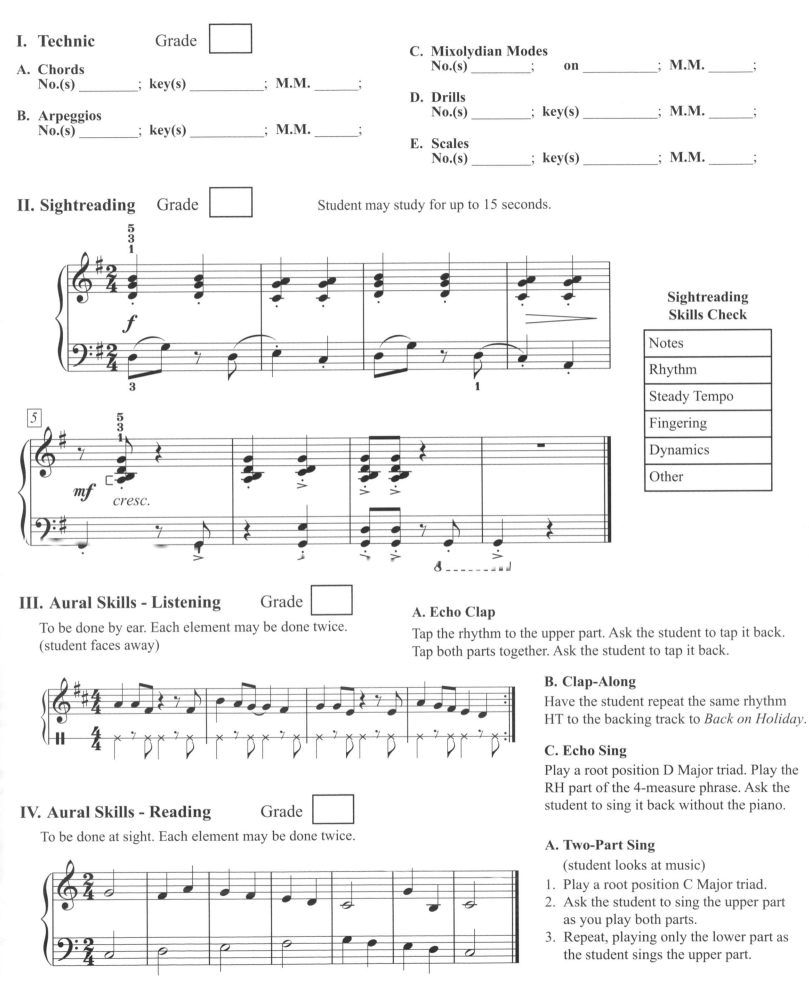

Sightreading Skills Check

Notes
Rhythm
Steady Tempo
Fingering
Dynamics
Other

III. Aural Skills - Listening Grade ☐

To be done by ear. Each element may be done twice. (student faces away)

A. Echo Clap

Tap the rhythm to the upper part. Ask the student to tap it back. Tap both parts together. Ask the student to tap it back.

B. Clap-Along

Have the student repeat the same rhythm HT to the backing track to *Back on Holiday*.

C. Echo Sing

Play a root position D Major triad. Play the RH part of the 4-measure phrase. Ask the student to sing it back without the piano.

IV. Aural Skills - Reading Grade ☐

To be done at sight. Each element may be done twice.

A. Two-Part Sing

(student looks at music)
1. Play a root position C Major triad.
2. Ask the student to sing the upper part as you play both parts.
3. Repeat, playing only the lower part as the student sings the upper part.

Unit 2 - Midterm

I. Technic   Grade ☐

A. Chords
No.(s) _____; key(s) _____; M.M. _____;

B. Arpeggios
No.(s) _____; key(s) _____; M.M. _____;

C. Mixolydian Modes
No.(s) _____;   on _____; M.M. _____;

D. Drills
No.(s) _____; key(s) _____; M.M. _____;

E. Scales
No.(s) _____; key(s) _____; M.M. _____;

II. Sightreading   Grade ☐   Student may study for up to 15 seconds.

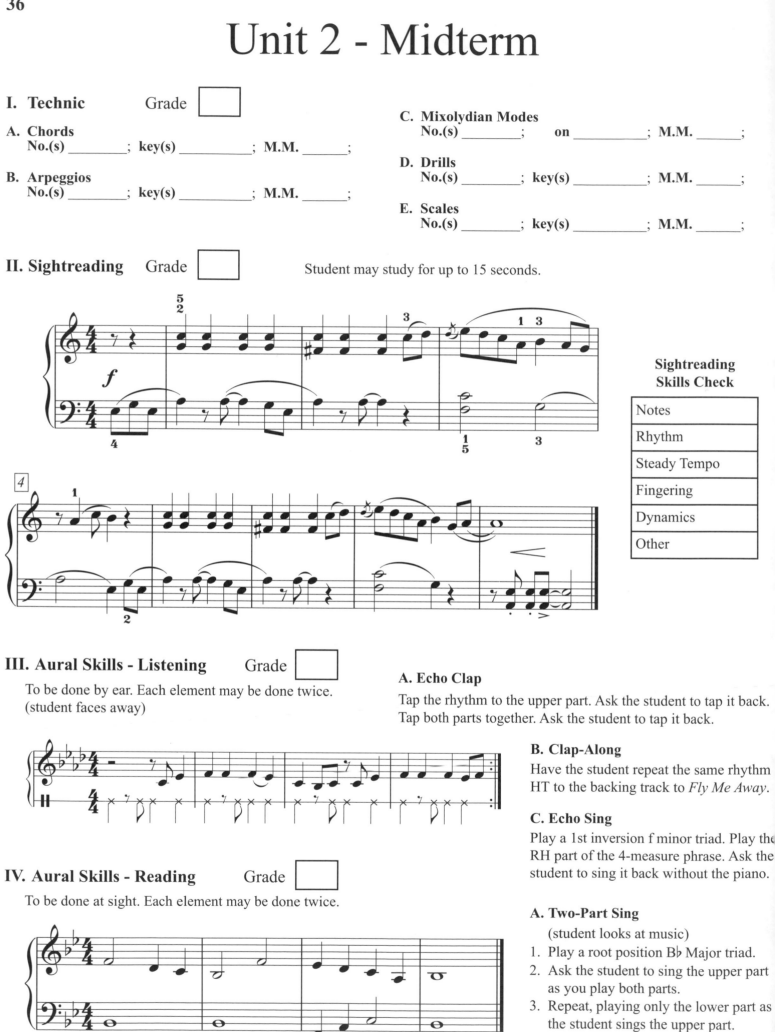

Sightreading Skills Check

Notes
Rhythm
Steady Tempo
Fingering
Dynamics
Other

III. Aural Skills - Listening   Grade ☐

To be done by ear. Each element may be done twice. (student faces away)

A. Echo Clap

Tap the rhythm to the upper part. Ask the student to tap it back. Tap both parts together. Ask the student to tap it back.

B. Clap-Along

Have the student repeat the same rhythm HT to the backing track to *Fly Me Away.*

C. Echo Sing

Play a 1st inversion f minor triad. Play the RH part of the 4-measure phrase. Ask the student to sing it back without the piano.

IV. Aural Skills - Reading   Grade ☐

To be done at sight. Each element may be done twice.

A. Two-Part Sing

(student looks at music)
1. Play a root position B♭ Major triad.
2. Ask the student to sing the upper part as you play both parts.
3. Repeat, playing only the lower part as the student sings the upper part.

Unit 2 - Final

I. Technic   Grade ☐

A. Chords
No.(s) _____ ; key(s) _____ ; M.M. _____ ;

B. Arpeggios
No.(s) _____ ; key(s) _____ ; M.M. _____ ;

C. Mixolydian Modes
No.(s) _____ ;   on _____ ; M.M. _____ ;

D. Drills
No.(s) _____ ; key(s) _____ ; M.M. _____ ;

E. Scales
No.(s) _____ ; key(s) _____ ; M.M. _____ ;

II. Sightreading   Grade ☐   Student may study for up to 15 seconds.

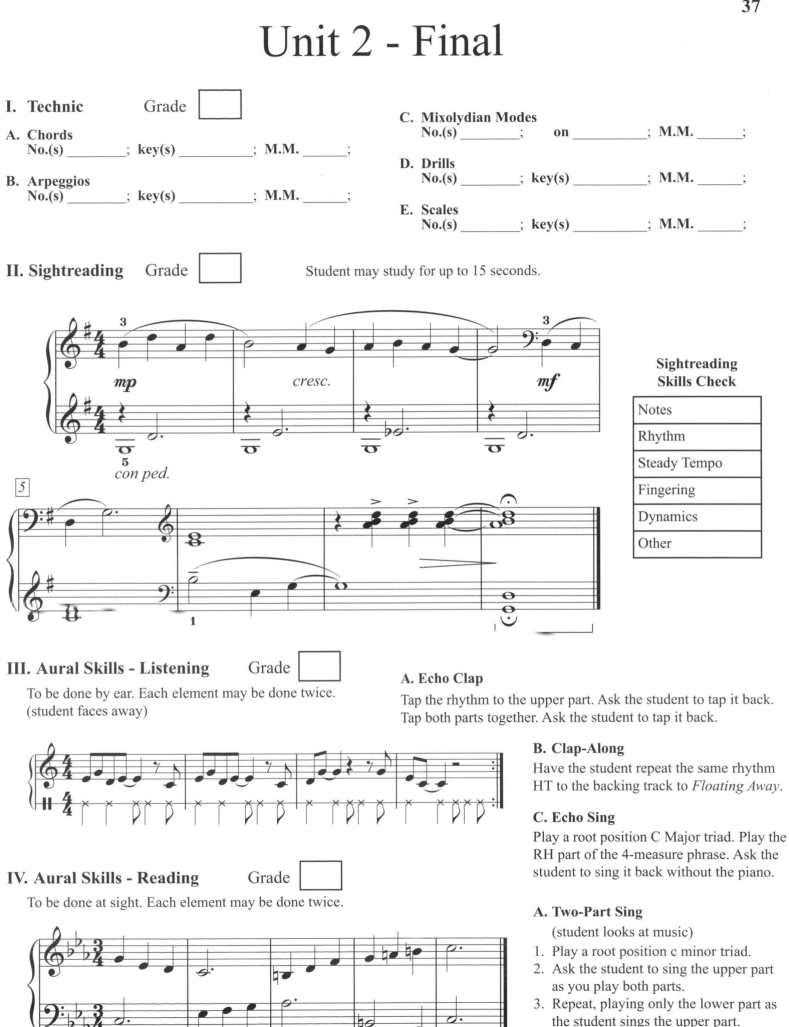

Sightreading Skills Check

Notes
Rhythm
Steady Tempo
Fingering
Dynamics
Other

III. Aural Skills - Listening   Grade ☐

To be done by ear. Each element may be done twice.
(student faces away)

A. Echo Clap

Tap the rhythm to the upper part. Ask the student to tap it back. Tap both parts together. Ask the student to tap it back.

B. Clap-Along

Have the student repeat the same rhythm HT to the backing track to *Floating Away.*

C. Echo Sing

Play a root position C Major triad. Play the RH part of the 4-measure phrase. Ask the student to sing it back without the piano.

IV. Aural Skills - Reading   Grade ☐

To be done at sight. Each element may be done twice.

A. Two-Part Sing

(student looks at music)

1. Play a root position c minor triad.
2. Ask the student to sing the upper part as you play both parts.
3. Repeat, playing only the lower part as the student sings the upper part.

Unit 3 - Midterm

I. Technic   Grade ☐

A. Chords
No.(s) _____ ;   key(s) _____ ;   M.M. _____ ;

B. Arpeggios
No.(s) _____ ;   key(s) _____ ;   M.M. _____ ;

C. Mixolydian Modes
No.(s) _____ ;   on _____ ;   M.M. _____ ;

D. Drills
No.(s) _____ ;   key(s) _____ ;   M.M. _____ ;

E. Scales
No.(s) _____ ;   key(s) _____ ;   M.M. _____ ;

II. Sightreading   Grade ☐   Student may study for up to 15 seconds.

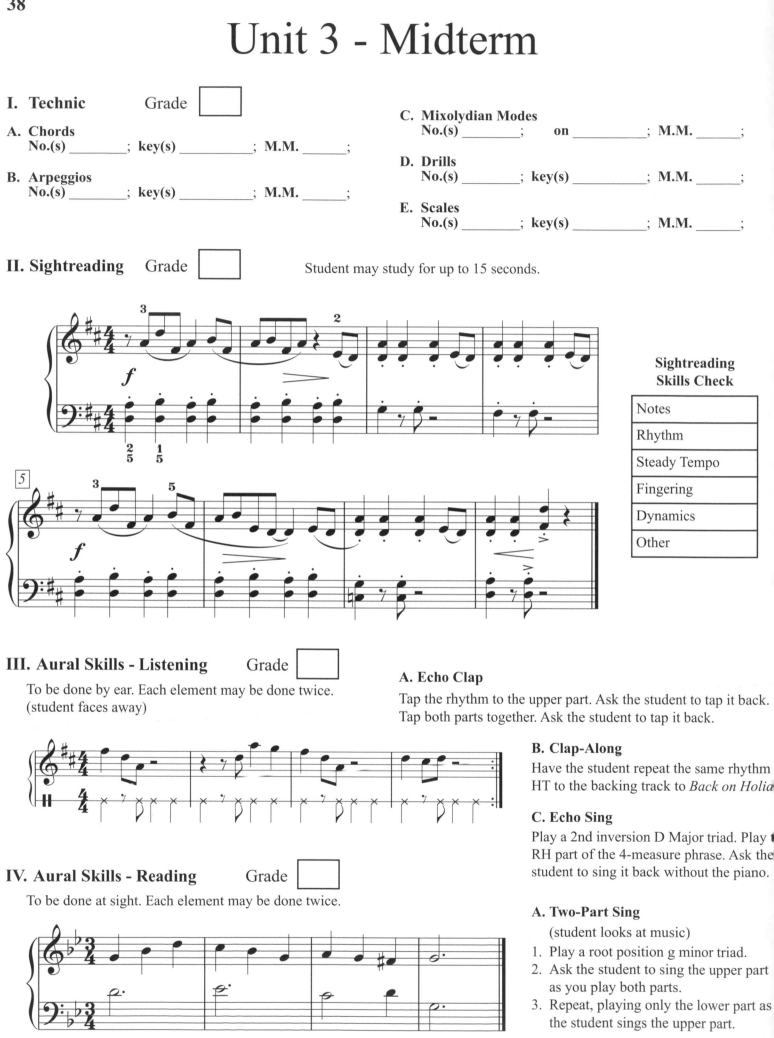

Sightreading Skills Check
Notes
Rhythm
Steady Tempo
Fingering
Dynamics
Other

III. Aural Skills - Listening   Grade ☐

To be done by ear. Each element may be done twice. (student faces away)

A. Echo Clap

Tap the rhythm to the upper part. Ask the student to tap it back. Tap both parts together. Ask the student to tap it back.

B. Clap-Along

Have the student repeat the same rhythm HT to the backing track to *Back on Holida*

C. Echo Sing

Play a 2nd inversion D Major triad. Play RH part of the 4-measure phrase. Ask the student to sing it back without the piano.

IV. Aural Skills - Reading   Grade ☐

To be done at sight. Each element may be done twice.

A. Two-Part Sing

(student looks at music)

1. Play a root position g minor triad.
2. Ask the student to sing the upper part as you play both parts.
3. Repeat, playing only the lower part as the student sings the upper part.

Unit 3 - Final

I. Technic   Grade [   ]

A. Chords
No.(s) _____ ; key(s) _____ ; M.M. _____ ;

B. Arpeggios
No.(s) _____ ; key(s) _____ ; M.M. _____ ;

C. Mixolydian Modes
No.(s) _____ ;   on _____ ; M.M. _____ ;

D. Drills
No.(s) _____ ; key(s) _____ ; M.M. _____ ;

E. Scales
No.(s) _____ ; key(s) _____ ; M.M. _____ ;

II. Sightreading   Grade [   ]   Student may study for up to 15 seconds.

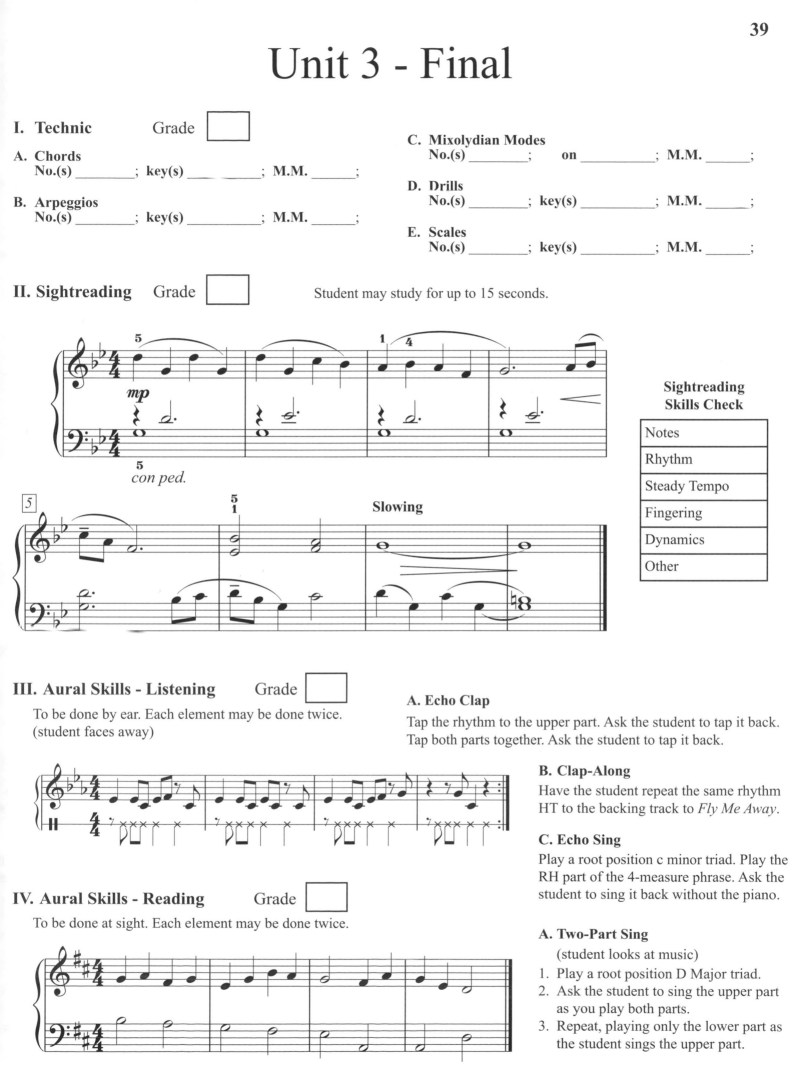

Sightreading Skills Check

Notes
Rhythm
Steady Tempo
Fingering
Dynamics
Other

III. Aural Skills - Listening   Grade [   ]

To be done by ear. Each element may be done twice. (student faces away)

IV. Aural Skills - Reading   Grade [   ]

To be done at sight. Each element may be done twice.

A. Echo Clap

Tap the rhythm to the upper part. Ask the student to tap it back. Tap both parts together. Ask the student to tap it back.

B. Clap-Along

Have the student repeat the same rhythm HT to the backing track to *Fly Me Away*.

C. Echo Sing

Play a root position c minor triad. Play the RH part of the 4-measure phrase. Ask the student to sing it back without the piano.

A. Two-Part Sing

(student looks at music)

1. Play a root position D Major triad.
2. Ask the student to sing the upper part as you play both parts.
3. Repeat, playing only the lower part as the student sings the upper part.

Unit 4 - Midterm

I. Technic   Grade ☐

A. Chords
No.(s) _____ ; key(s) _____ ; M.M. _____ ;

B. Arpeggios
No.(s) _____ ; key(s) _____ ; M.M. _____ ;

C. Mixolydian Modes
No.(s) _____ ;   on _____ ; M.M. _____ ;

D. Drills
No.(s) _____ ; key(s) _____ ; M.M. _____ ;

E. Scales
No.(s) _____ ; key(s) _____ ; M.M. _____ ;

II. Sightreading   Grade ☐   Student may study for up to 15 seconds.

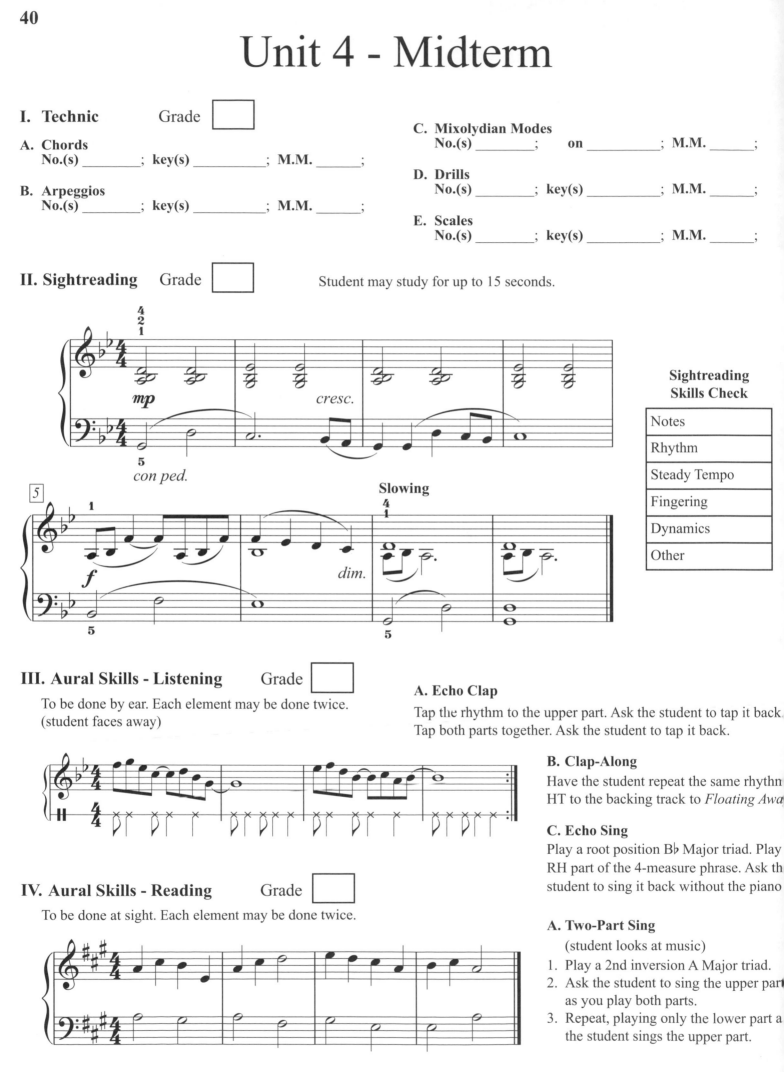

Sightreading Skills Check
Notes
Rhythm
Steady Tempo
Fingering
Dynamics
Other

III. Aural Skills - Listening   Grade ☐

To be done by ear. Each element may be done twice.
(student faces away)

A. Echo Clap

Tap the rhythm to the upper part. Ask the student to tap it back.
Tap both parts together. Ask the student to tap it back.

B. Clap-Along

Have the student repeat the same rhythm
HT to the backing track to *Floating Awa*

C. Echo Sing

Play a root position B♭ Major triad. Play
RH part of the 4-measure phrase. Ask th
student to sing it back without the piano

IV. Aural Skills - Reading   Grade ☐

To be done at sight. Each element may be done twice.

A. Two-Part Sing

(student looks at music)

1. Play a 2nd inversion A Major triad.
2. Ask the student to sing the upper par
   as you play both parts.
3. Repeat, playing only the lower part a
   the student sings the upper part.

Unit 4 - Final

41

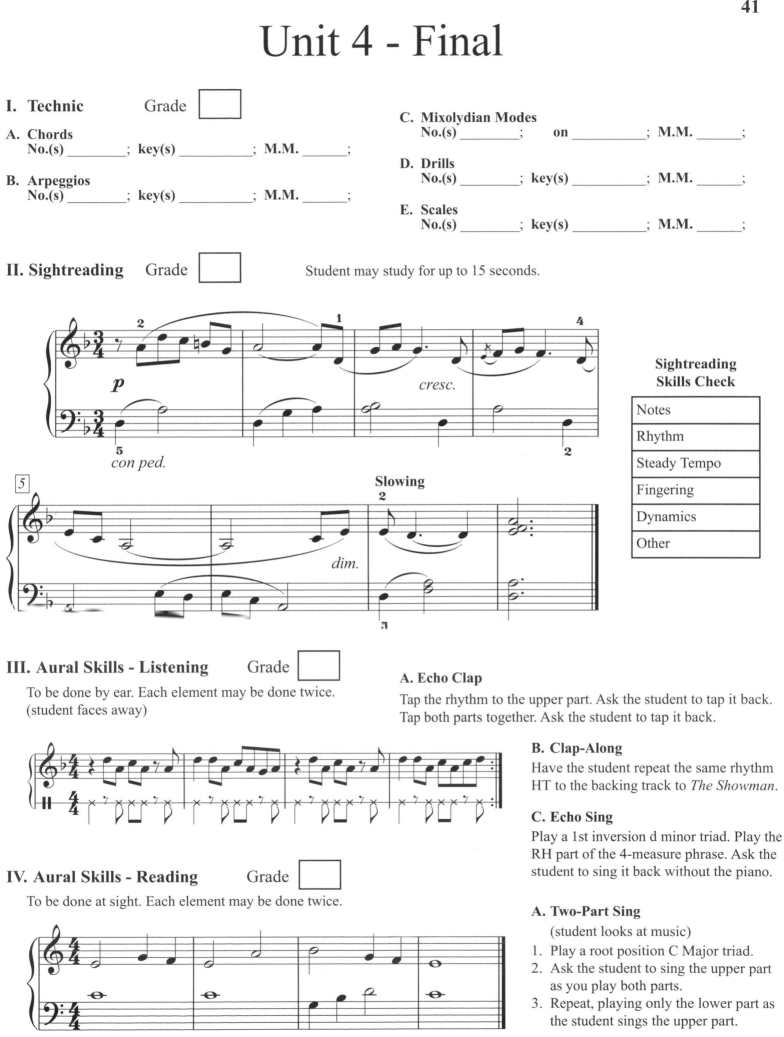

I. Technic   Grade ☐

A. Chords
No.(s) _____; key(s) _____; M.M. _____;

B. Arpeggios
No.(s) _____; key(s) _____; M.M. _____;

C. Mixolydian Modes
No.(s) _____;   on _____; M.M. _____;

D. Drills
No.(s) _____; key(s) _____; M.M. _____;

E. Scales
No.(s) _____; key(s) _____; M.M. _____;

II. Sightreading   Grade ☐   Student may study for up to 15 seconds.

p   cresc.   con ped.

Sightreading Skills Check

| Notes |
| Rhythm |
| Steady Tempo |
| Fingering |
| Dynamics |
| Other |

Slowing   dim.

III. Aural Skills - Listening   Grade ☐

To be done by ear. Each element may be done twice. (student faces away)

A. Echo Clap
Tap the rhythm to the upper part. Ask the student to tap it back. Tap both parts together. Ask the student to tap it back.

B. Clap-Along
Have the student repeat the same rhythm HT to the backing track to *The Showman*.

C. Echo Sing
Play a 1st inversion d minor triad. Play the RH part of the 4-measure phrase. Ask the student to sing it back without the piano.

IV. Aural Skills - Reading   Grade ☐

To be done at sight. Each element may be done twice.

A. Two-Part Sing
(student looks at music)
1. Play a root position C Major triad.
2. Ask the student to sing the upper part as you play both parts.
3. Repeat, playing only the lower part as the student sings the upper part.

Level 5 Scales

Stop-and-Go Scales

1. Right Hand
   a) What notes does your thumb play? _____, _____
   b) What note does your 4th finger play? _____

2. Left Hand
   a) What notes does your thumb play? _____, _____
   b) What note does your 4th finger play? _____

3. Look at Exercise No. 1 below. Fill in the blanks with the correct finger number.

4. Play Exercise No. 1. At each fermata, STOP and say the finger and note name for the next note in the hand that is crossing over or under. For example, in m. 1 pause on beat 2 and say "1 on F", referring to the next note in the RH, then continue to the next fermata (beat 3, m. 1).

Basic Patterns

Play 5x times a day, increasing the speed slightly every day or two, at your teacher's direction.

Complementary Patterns

Play 5x times a day, increasing the speed slightly every day or two, at your teacher's direction.

No. 4   ♩ = 50 - 80

No. 5   ♩ = 50 - 80

No. 6   ♩ = 50 - 80

No. 7   ♩ = 50 - 80

Level 5 Chords

Cadences

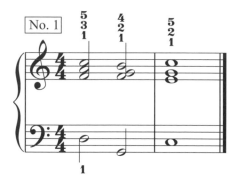

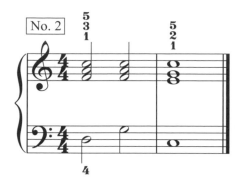

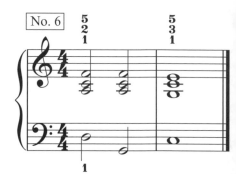

Chords

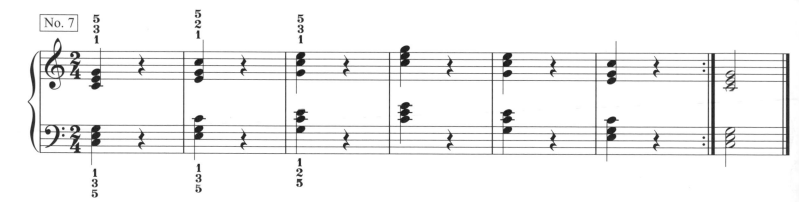

No. 9

No. 10

No. 11

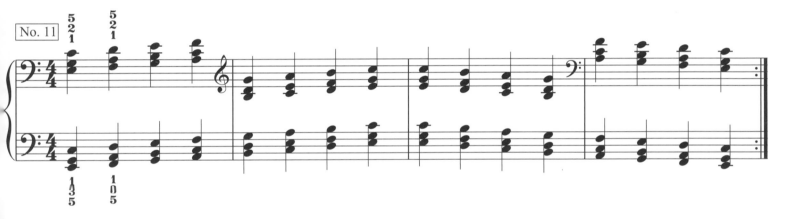

No. 12

No. 13

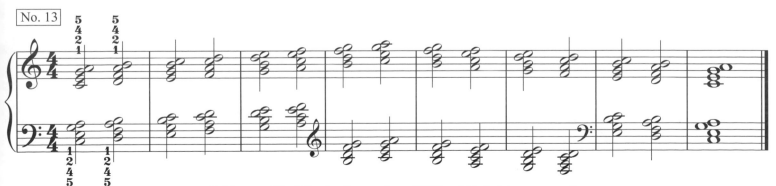

46

Level 5 Arpeggios

No. 1

No. 2

No. 3

Level 5 Mixolydian Mode & Licks

A Mixolydian Mode is a scale that has half steps between scale degrees 3–4 and 6–7. You can think of it as a major scale with a lowered 7th. For example, the "C Mixolydian" is like a C Major scale, only with a B♭:
1. Start with a major scale;
2. Lower the 7th scale degree a half step.

Level 5 Drills

Drawbridge / Rotation Exercises

1. Preparation

Lift your arm about 3 inches above the key without bending at the wrist – as if it were a drawbridge. Flex your starting finger so it feels strong (in m.1, your fifth finger, in m.2 your fourth finger, etc.).

2. Sound Production

a) Play each whole note by dropping into the key, releasing your arm weight with energy. Your wrist should not drop below key level.

b) For each quarter note, without releasing the whole note:
   i. Rotate toward the finger holding the whole note;
   ii. Rotate back "down" into position, using this motion to create the sound;
   iii. Repeat for each quarter note.

3. Follow Through

Repeat from the beginning on each new whole note.

Upstroke / Inward Rotation Exercises

1. Preparation

Rest your hand on the surface of the keys in good position.

2. Sound Production

a) Play the first note and all the following pickup notes by gently swinging "in" to "stand up" on your thumb. The upward motion creates the sound on the pickup notes.

b) At the same time, rotate your hand towards the thumb to prepare for the accented notes:
   i. Your thumb position changes from parallel to the key to a comfortably upright position;
   ii. The end of the thumb rotates from the side of the thumb halfway to the tip;

   iii. While the thumb is "standing", the other fingers also lift, opening your hand;
   iv. Relax your hand and arm.

c) "Fall down" to create the sound on the accented notes. You should feel the sensation of falling, dropping, and release.

d) For the accented ♩ notes in mm. 10-11 and 13-14, continue to hold each note as you "stand up" to prepare the next note. Then "fall down" on the next ♩ note to create the sound, as above.

e) Return your hand to level and repeat the process.

Upstroke / Outward Rotation Exercises

1. Preparation
Rest your hand on the surface of the keys in good position.

2. Sound Production

a) Play the first note and all the following pickup notes by swinging "in" to "stand up" on your fifth finger. The upward motion creates the sound on the pickup notes.

b) At the same time, rotate your hand towards the fifth finger to prepare for the accented notes:

    i. Your finger position changes from parallel to the key to a comfortably upright position;

    ii. The end of the finger rotates from the pad of the finger almost to the tip;

    iii. While the fifth finger is "standing", the other fingers also lift, opening your hand;

    iv. Relax your hand and arm.

c) "Fall down" to create the sound on the accented notes. You should feel the sensation of falling, dropping, and release.

d) For the accented ♩ notes in mm. 10-11 and 13-14, continue to hold each note as you "stand up" to prepare the next note. Then "fall down" on the next ♩ note to create the sound, as above.

e) Return your hand to level and repeat the process.

How to Use This Book

The *American Popular Piano Skills* books are designed to be used as a flexible tool for learning the fundamental skills of playing the piano. Research tells us that the most effective way to learn is in small increments, repeated frequently. That's a good thing, considering that many piano students today have very busy schedules and may not have big chunks of time to devote to practice at one time.

How much time should you spend on basic skills? The best choice, of course, is to spend a moderate amount of time daily on technic, sightreading and ear training. But even a smaller amount of time each day, every day is better than spending a lot of time on one day after several days of non-practice.

The Open Plan System

The Open Plan organization of the *American Popular Piano Skills* books encourages skill acquisition at each student's natural pace. Review the chart below to help understand how it works.

How should you schedule assignments of Skills? Progress will vary depending on each student's needs and practice timetable.

- **Faster moving students** can do one module per week.
- **Many students** will work on two or three skill areas within a module each week.
- **Students with less practice time** often do just one skill area.

Areas that need extra work may of course be repeated as necessary.

American Popular Piano
Skills Book-Level Five

Four Learning Units		Four Examination Units	
to be done by the student at home		to be administered by the teacher at the lesson	
Each Unit contains:		Each Unit contains:	
4 Learning Modules Each module covers the following skill areas:		**2 Tests** **Midterm:** to be completed after Module 2 **Final:** to be completed after Module 4	
Technic	Chords, arpeggios, Mixolydian modes, drills, and scales; along with rhythmic, dynamic, and articulation variants	**Technic**	Chords Arpeggios Mixolydian Modes Drills Scales
Prepared Sightreading	A short musical excerpt	**Sightreading**	Short examples, with skills checklist
Aural Skills– Rhythmic	Rhythm clapping in two parts	**Aural Skills– Listening**	Echo Clap Clap-Along Echo Sing
Aural Skills– Pitch	Sing-along, two-part interval sing	**Aural Skills– Reading**	Two-Part Interval Sing

Some Basic Tips

Singing Vocalizing has not always been part of traditional piano lessons. Yet recent research has clearly established its importance for developing crucial listening and audiating skills.

Teaching and learning singing in this context is not hard, but does take patience. Many students have not sung and will need some time and work in order to get comfortable. Stick with it! Studies have shown that even those who seem totally tone-deaf on the first attempt can improve significantly with practice.

- Check that posture is good, breathing deep and even, and throat relaxed.
- If the student is having trouble matching pitch, ask them to sing a note and hold it. Find the same pitch and sing it with them. Then ask them to move their voice with you as you sing to the correct pitch.
- Visual and verbal feedback is crucial. Saying "higher" or "lower", or moving your hand up or down to help them find the pitch is a great help.

Technic Technic should be practiced daily. Vary the focus of each week's assignment using the Technic Box in each Module.

- **Fill in the blanks** for the metronome marking (M.M.) and the number of the exercise.
- **Circle** the chosen key(s), articulation(s), and dynamic(s).

Technical exercises are set out in a single key in the last few pages of this book. For students who work better from a printed page, consider using the *Level 5 Technic Book* for the other keys.

Sightreading The word "sightreading" is a misnomer; a better term might be "pattern recognition" or even "flash learning". A good sightreader recognizes familiar patterns in new arrangements; he or she is able to think ahead, keep going despite mistakes, and keep a steady beat.

Here are some steps that have helped my students improve their sightreading:

- Play the piece at a slow tempo without stopping. After finishing, go back and circle mistakes. This builds both analysis and musical memory skills.
- Play slowly again and try to fix all the mistakes – and not add any new ones!
- Play a third time, counting out loud. This time it should be error free.

Steps may be repeated as necessary.

Mix Do you have to do all the activities for every section? You'll make the right decision based on available time, skill level and long-term goals. Remember, the most important factor in improving fundamentals is: **work on them — and do it often!!**